Keats Is Not the Problem

Poems

Brett Evans and Christopher Shipman

Lavender Ink
lavenderink.org

Library of Congress Control Number: 2017962690
Evans, Brett and Christopher Shipman
Keats Is Not the Problem / Brett Evans and Christopher Shipman;
p. cm.
ISBN: 978-1-944884-36-9 (pbk.)

Lavender Ink
lavenderink.org

Acknowledgements

Grateful acknowledgment is made to the publications in which versions of the following poems first appeared (sometimes with different titles):

"Arkansas Summer Chimera" and "Dana Play Dough" *Fell Swoop*

"At Last the Meaning of Halloween Stickers!" *Haiku Journal*

"Hush Now, Henrietta," "Last Call," "Sleep-Light Advice" "Mother I'm Sorry" *Spork Press*

"Night Man: Ep.1," "Henrietta did it, in the kitchen, with her dreams," "O Henrietta! O Mother! O Meaning!," "Henrietta's Delicious and Compact Body" *Tender-loin*

"Princes and Charmers," "Roach Giant," "Keats is Not the Problem," "Bowie Second Line," "In the Hopeful Future," "Weathering," "Bereavement Myth" *Unlikely Stories*

A special thanks to the Poem-A-Day crew, in whose April or November some of these poems were first composed.

And a very special thanks to Rodger Kamenetz, Amber Qureshi and Todd Shrenk for lending their words to our words, and to Caleb McIntosh for allowing the color and shape of his madness to cover ours in the storm of what comes…

Keats Is Not the Problem

KEATS IS NOT THE PROBLEM

MEANINGFUL POEMS

BERRYMAN VS BERRIGAN: THE BOARDGAME

the Xmas after her brother's death   143

DEDICATIONS

Poems require no maintenance

so I took a poem
from the pill drawer
read it left it
took a pill
and some money
and started to write
some more

POEMS FROM THE PILL DRAWER

Aging in America (When the Music's Not Quite Over)

It's weird to think
    some people got
    old and died
before the apocalypse hit

Who Killed the World?
on the celestial seasonings
 tea flap, beer bib

and what about geriatric
    roaches who just age out
of scurrying living

and flaming hot Funyons
 besting nuclear winters

 hearts on the fire
like terminal marshmallows.

psst— Spring is about youthiness
                    and bed springs

but once I read with the poet
 Stephen Rodefer

at the 13 Bar in New York,
    he among younger poets
    reading about sorrows of the flesh

even though we poets are supposed
    to be like opera singers time-
  wise, relative to peak.

Aging in America is one thing
Dying in Paris is another
so Andy, yeah—

being young
  shucked smushed upright
    in a Pittsburgh flat just might
be roundly where it's at

or just flying a kite on a field
    before they invented
    all this shit that killed us

platform kids

huff glue
outside the movies
looney tunes glue
until shut-eye
pacifier rags
there are no pacifiers
atoms for peace
who made this place
this place?

wake up
wipe the glue crust
from corner mouth
start all over again
make the sale
be your own
runaway
in place

stuck

(Chasers)

Acadian Ambulance Services presents
Cowboy Mouth
or, better,
in bridge traffic
"Bring on the Dancing Horses" regresses

to the tastier "Never Stop"
watching the hatchback
use the sudden ambulance sirens
as an excuse to jostle
six positions up

Spring has sprung
but someone somewhere's
fallen over or something
Life pairs well with the Other Thing

anything beats Wagner's Meats
                                    if you let it

anything's better than
Morris Bart
presents   Bag of Donuts

gawk

at the airport a young mom
grabs her fat toddler
by the mohawk

I wish I was gawking up at her
I wish I was loving her

shiny thighs like two
orphaned moonbeams
shot from her cutoffs

learning how to breathe in fear
expel anything like love

I am somewhere else
under another sea
of people passing by

but I wish I was her angry fish
flopping on the floor
for all to gawk at

Roach Giant

And after I just see the
are you kidding me? -size
cockroach, somehow not
fleeing the scything foot,
then I see why– he's a roach
with a fuzzball sidecar!

got a fuzzball sidecar tagalong
anchor weight in nano-ounces
yet enough to lame him
as he ouijas to the corner
behind clawfoot tub
and I'm suddenly sympathetic

I too have started mornings
with kites made of lead
flying off foot, pushing a big
lint racket up the mountain
blowing my own levee
ruining for the hills

        I go into the next room
        and write these lines down

        He appears again!
        as I return to the bathroom
        & just after I had written
        the previous sympathy bit
        he now flagrantly forces the kill

I return with paper towel
but when going in for said kill
he goes belly-up
and does the ill-pickle
leg-wiggle thing

so half against my will again
with the towel
I perform a fuzzball-ectomy
(just last week I lost a dog)
and send him on his way

mints for the cadets

new battlefield
has its own airfield
and racetrack
  and tracking app

    way to move corpse gamepieces
      less your gran's gig economy
        more free beer warm fluid

    bridge treated like party barge but

we need to cross this   onto any far out metropolis
that will have us   welcome night skin lullaby

          it can't be too late
          to get a pet
                  door or adopt
          Janis Joplin

                    the general feeling
                    out in the country

        over the rhythm sticks
        she put a giggling armada
        a caterwaul
                  train tracks on the moon

          turns out artillery shells
          benefit this butterfly

defeated the war
before it cd even
get started
losing herself too

heart muscle card

delivered by ancient
blimp & stick method
I find out
we are in
mines of the business
be all birds and bees
rock-climbing prodigies
with a taste for starter dirt
candy wag of the stand of
pines in the breeze
be mine heart [.......] it said
& we'll have a picnic up top
discern gods in the knees
and shoulder blades
if love is aloft in gneiss & cirrus
if sweaty yeti do exist

_____

[optional last lines]

sweat like rubies on her
wobble-tunable upper lip

fear of flying

the larger the fear
the smaller the plane

        sitting next to me
        fear disguised as a woman

from a small town in Arkansas
near where I grew tall—

which is somewhere outside the window

past the propeller blade with other fears I
pay no attention to

past the center of that black mechanism
        that perpetual birth
      of black circles that big

black bullet spinning always toward more
air more cloud more sky
        always more
        that gigantic
more
    that pointy
        that nipple

always erect   always a desire to be
always sucked

always a mother
always

a winged murderer—   a lustful passenger

meaning well

staring through the window
terrified of its glass and that gassy air
and its promise of absence

like the man in front of us

his fear

larger than his talk of god
terrified

that there could be a god other than him

and me
of the possibility
that a complimentary cup

of coffee

can put this all to rest
as long as the latest James Bond
falling out of the sky
on the in-flight film

promises to land on his feet

Aztec Camera

I've noticed in my travels that a nail gun
is one thing impossible to sleep through,
whether it's Spudly's or Irish famine in
the belly, the longest short cut broken rule.

So call mom on the phone and break her
Saturday shopping algorithm, purse slung
against the sun if it's getting cross, making
a stew out of organs and bargains

nothing to make Orpheus get anyone
back from the dead for, but not exactly
boot leather either. Smart in her car coat,
she still has a way of coming out on top.

Almonaster Blvd. with its jalopy-vom of cars
rattles the dream she had in mind, as it did/
does to mine, so I'm smashed against this hill
with Katya, unpacking our just-packed bags.

Almost home

I think of things to call the clouds,
like Wonder Woman bath foam,

Santa chins—I don't know, a few other
shitty things, but it doesn't matter.

I feel really shitty anyway, and
we'll be on the ground momentarily

is crackling through the intercom.
I'd rather be back in the shitty place

I'd walked for three days to escape
the question I can't quit asking myself:

*How long could this plane fly before
inevitably crashing?* But before

I know it the plane is landing safely;
the clouds are someone else's problem.

Gone missing

She wore a beige sleeveless tunic top
she was of two minds and just one body

Casey is (right) one amazing woman–
having been brought up in a family of mechanics,
she decided to continue with the same work.
She has always impressed her clients
due to her resilience and clean work.

But now she has gone missing
where it's less safe to streetcar or walk than drive.

This city can be a real shit, or far worse.

Natural woman looking snazzy and roaming
because Sunday programming tends to suck
can't still get you... sadly, we just don't know.
Taking the grease off bit by bit and peeling
into a dress can still scent-stick the monsters

that pass for boring citizens. Some just can't
leave the Land of the Living alone, for the good.

She wore a beige sleeveless tunic top, black ballet flats
and blue jeans, and carried a blue purse by Michael Kors.

{ the murmur of terror }

on the radio
tells me it's Wednesday

what a withering eye
can't gather
a heart can un-hold

its grip on things
reduced to aorta, fluids,
and wires
on the subway floor

starter-screams & groans
achieving at last
the human uni-language
promised in the space programs

class,

I want to get back
to the tulip markets failing

fucking folly of man
but at least with some beauty
as its starting point

as with
woman   snake
ships   hips

the forest

the simmering fog stolls
the Mull of Kintyre
and Boggy Creek
                    alike

or we could just have a blast
this Spring Break
have some in and out burgers
with the news we can get
get so super off

Nola Still Life no. 1

dude on bicycle

on one of those Walkman

talk out loud phones

talking about money

coming from the bayou

weather a dash

pre-hurricaney

Nola Still Life no. 2

neutral ground grassy shadow

silver bike chained

painted ghost freshly sprayed

blue-shirted black kids

yellow buckets

pails undiminished by absence

of shovel or sand

fifth driver mimics every lip

shut white by sweat

no eyes open wide

money's a meaningful mouth

money shot heard round the world

caught up in the likes

friend periscopes friend

getting the forcible treatment

with very little style points

and bleaker outlook for future soul

Us,

we don't want to get basted

by any Mary Quants

in British submarines

We'll be hosed by our own heroes

and live stream our own goal

Uncertain Dates the new frontier

Next up: the eroticization of Camden
Next up: hardcore charcuterie

Caught up in the likes =

the new   I didn't want to get involved

Caution: do not consume oxygen absorber
Caution: do not be born after certain date

from Revolution to basic arc

the Republic became unjust = just a jit in the dark

$1000 goodbye

I can still apex the bridge
and see W Bank refinery puffs
as de Chirico paintings, yes?

Think about Johnny's
rad pre-Chaz Fest
pancake party?

but then it's back to gloom.
In another one
for the Carcinogen Follies

K-Doe, black dog,
has melanoma, moving all around
fairly fast

the thousand dollars we thought
was fixing something only
stop-gapped, took some teeth out

bought time
borrowed time
lost the house

feeling petty even thinking about
money but that particular annoying
alloy bonds strongly to pain

force-multiplies

anything else
going wrong.

So what's left but
The Parting Friend Workout Routine

up and down the ramp
to the backyard once a playground
ruddering the handle-harness

really crack that 6-pack
and rock out
with your back out–

I can only makes gallows jokes
because my prayer skills suck

and if I start crying
I end up George and Tammy

splitting the blanket
with a whip and dead air.

K has been a great friend.
The most normal, funny, no-fuss
dog's dog imaginable–

super necessary as our others
have been lovable bitches and ninnies
needing the sturdy companion.

Despite our seeming speck-fulness
so many of us are completely
irreplaceable, some even moreso.

Losing dog, the block, New Orleans, National
Parks, the milky way, the universe

white and black holes
but not the hole in my   [rhymes with tart].

In most of de Chirico's melancholy vistas
there's rarely ever human or beast

so we're both written out
of the picture for now

but like anybody has to think
maybe not forever.

Late-Night Lift-Off

a fat yellow fig is
in the branches of the moon
and I'm reminded
of the three compliments I got
on the walk—
front porch to Rite Aid
to front porch—
for the box combo of Huggies
and Pabst and
how it was not enough
to exit the tragic actor so stag
in every bar window
as I passed— singing dis
and dat catharsis

{ the uncraving }

—*after Buck*

the first night of the frogs
was the last day
I quit smoking.
Go slow with the South,

but not in that way.
(Like 'SoFag' [a new real estate
coinage– 'South of Fairgrounds']
does a really nice gloaming.

Y cabeza. Super playback.
Like, why do I hate
the lack of want to do bad?
Not a bucket list on belt but

'buckets' with a lisp–
bailing everything–
These poems are terribly
fun to write. It beats

interior lighting
supplied by Check Engine
so radio louder. The grass
on the levee is something

I don't have to tend–
it tends itself, like the river

a hundred years ago. This uncraving
will just have to do.

Vampires on AARP just
catching some rays. & thus
no more need to triple park,
double down, or single myself

out for lack of angelhood again.
Dear Chris, hello. I am working
on this rad good greeting,
and the frogs just can't

say enough about it, you.

Bowie Second Line

hard to say if we both believed
Bowie died for our sins

when the woman
who had been heavy-breathing
her wild mom-breath

into the kitchen cabinets
all morning

slid into the living room
wearing her best Bowie dress
to find me uncertain—

is a couch is a sleeping baby
or a sleeping baby a couch?

either way it seemed
reason enough to call for a sitter
either way something dead

inside us was squirming
in its heavy sleep

either way the New Orleans sky
hung above
the crowd in the Quarter

like a sheet falling slowly over
a baby, or glitter on a couch

parole

    summer get me
     housey & lightly
manic

palimpsesting on all /
allover   the phantom
     swimwear

so shake

yr Pensa-
          cola, hula

   "we can't survive
    on yr bedroom eyes"

alone

Sunday Morning in New Orleans

In other dreams of America
autumn is signing its trees over
to the sky's contradiction.

Here in New Orleans my mind is
fettered to the failing gate
that surrounds my house.

Outside it the free newspapers
are matted with rain
to the orange bags holding them.

Across the street
in the neighbor's attic rats run
from a drill bit's impossible noise.

I'm sure the Saints will lose.
Even behind closed eyes a black
cloud hangs in the sky

like something dead for days.

getting rained on

with my old dog

we can't run home anymore!

raindrops rather cold

for N.O. this time of year

I envision

toweling her off

N.O.P.S.T

getting professionally developed
a week after grades
have been submitted and
comments written
for the cards

makes me feel sort of misplaced
something maybe
like a skull lost in a box
in the August attic
of an Air B&B

Notes for final poem afield Jass Fest

Air B&B my misery,
it's super authentic.

One more solid paper
& you're in A-ville.

One more sock
to yr blue movie B-side.

One more red
organizing the pickles

and we can all come together
as in come.

Going with Whitman
can make you more than

a sampler, so dining in Camden
and sharing-economy classes
(with passed chalice)

might just not hurt your
bottom but your bottom line.

Don't get bent.
You didn't make the game

you just tried to twain
Jeff Goldblum from the ointment.

funny space

                rainy foolscape
  not just for drivers
but for all ALL Orleanians–

   me coffee cloud fully saturated
I had to come home
   and gozzle down some orange julii
           for comfort

Dear Peshmerga,   you should try
               being this

               less dry

  Dear Balloon Institute,
     when I wanted to join this group again
         I stumbled on an old piece of mail
        that revealed my former

          view of the future,
         the man I trans am.

    I was literally on Flood St. today
     & needed a far better boogie board

      I needed a time machine mariner
      with both sass and class in spades

Show me your Weather v.

Sippy Cup Recall – Mold

Knife v. Uber

 PTZLA v. DXTNCNJ

  Birmingham Barons   v. Pensacola Blue Wahoos

I Got Frenchfaced
On Shitman Street

            & only got this lousy V-neck

Minor League Baseball v. Major Ling Bush

 Psst/ beekeeping was just her cover v.

        a towering pop-up

The beach is roughly just past
                right center field

The Uninviteds
became cherished

   swing for the fences friends

Reincarnation Therapy

the morning   after the morning
schools closed

        for the rain that didn't rain

I sit strange
in the living room

mourning the lost monster of rumor
as it drizzles

  blessing the water
      forecasted to crack the ceiling

even though nothing dumped
I want to splash in the puddles

I know I need to stay alive
I know I need to make angels   to be able

to learn to swim

      to be
        weird in the water

flapping wings like a couple of kids
out on a snow day for rain
that unfloods a path to the sun

of another New Orleans

                    but instead I sit
                    a stack of books

on the couch and couch
the baby beside it

to drown in the nearest womb
I borrow the baby's crayons
                              sheets

of scribbled paper and little seat

and draw the flower of invisibility
five times
to not have to give god
another name
to not have to give
                    anything anything

when Sarah rises from the withering
rose of her blanket

from the jolt
            of sleepless dreams

I give all I have to give
I fridge the flowers

and steal away to trim back my ears

      and feelies

but the barber shop is closed
Saturdays regardless of rain

      and the walk back is always

weird when even the weird
      political climate

      is fucking with my path
      to a better past life

to carry it to the cloud

pregnant with what
      comes next

anyway   the walk back is always
anyway

but back home the baby
goes down easy as a window
for watching rain

and Sarah glides through her grief
to find me outside

sliding from my chair

into the sky where I've been trying
to scribble in
                        a sun to hide behind

ready again to Cousteau off the side
of the front porch

but when she gets all electric
when she storms the invisible fence

                between us

to tell me about her new performance

when she says she'll grow wings
that
she'll shake the sky

then   thanks to scientists
listens to the sounds stars make
on her laptop

                        I'm inside that light

the noise of naming
            night anew

like a kind of front porch

reincarnation therapy
                    that lets in the rain

science is an amazing thing
                    but not

as amazing as us

KEATS IS NOT THE PROBLEM

Po and Proph

inelastic resources

together with the bursty nature
of dyadic communications

require elastic relief

weirdy enough this non-children's
film features a land line,

so will Jessica Bangkok
be your confidant?

will you stay chatty &
Fuck Hot Divorced?

in a three

with the two cuddle-cats
sporting that ideal 70s

kind of callipygous panache

the throwback ass is just
what the prophet ordered

After What Was is
the name of the jernt

sad bastard music

if the bad sads make sense
I want to use the word *suddenly*
to describe how the rain is your face

it's hard to find a song not about me
in this sort of selfishness
I mean the neighbor's schizophrenic

work on the wall of his shotgun
(hammer and saw and gunshot laughter)
is a metaphor for *my* life

I mean I keep waiting for you to fall
into a Pixies fire hole again—
touch this or that river with a dagger

even if I can't promise it won't melt
I mean I mean anyway *suddenly*
songs are making sense

Princes and Charmers

we felt fucking great
at the 1984 World's Fair

When Doves Cry

was one of our main jams
that summer

  & it wasn't your typical
teenage royalty
on the town situation

  after 10 the rides got cheap
and the loves got piled
onto laps and strapped in

for the lights and the music–
 the round and round
still a trip

the city still delightfully shitty
all by the water where it should be
     defiance in its best playful strain

  something about the clouds and us mixed

it never rained

       we did it again and again
         all summer

Fun and Games

The houses with people near
death have been replaced
by people with gauges.

Stops us not from jamming
across the Ouija boards
money shot planchette.

Dear Heavens
we are elastic and mystic
and mucho America

as in South
and Central
also known as The Taint

in Asperanto. We play Taint Tag
when our gizmos aren't working
and stream all the Tank Battles

We like stuff in our mouths
we heart hot rods
and POTUS.

We are the children
you had
on board.

The end credit music

is the best
it's end-times tangy.

For Nik in pander-flavor
we say Hey-ya!
For the Poem-a-Day players
we sing Keats in Space!
Hand me my hat and hands off
my Zardoz merkin!

For Jamie, we say
We bitter–
therefore we am.

For the Costco meatballs
that burned my roof– it was all
on a Mardi Gras Day.

My stroke of insight
the black kung fu experience

& three parting words–
ethanol potbelly pig.

Andy at the pool
   (male gaze goggle fire sale)

being immersed gives
him the *greenlight*
that alcohol used to
as in 'not having to'

just stay down and in
raisin in the water
fully dunked for an hour
and you cant drink or smoke

coming up
to strippers at the pool
ass in yr face tableau
can never be bad

in g strings
this one too big
this one too small but still
just average them in yr mind I suggest

his foster grants cant
tint out fast enough
to permit 'oogling' he says
'ogling' I think but don't correct him

Houseboat House

just because the flat screen
in the ladies room at La Carreta
was playing People's Court
just for Sarah
doesn't mean it wasn't
confusing

being there un-hungover
was enough to make me ask her
if she was okay

not the way I asked her
when she was leaning over
on her knees by the levee
when she reassured me she was
just looking
for a four leaf clover

but the way that being
in Baton Rouge and not feeling
like we could choose
the right color to carriage

our love like we used to could
made me have to ask
I mean we hadn't even chosen
a dish since the new menu
bloomed its plastic laminated
plumage

better to just order margaritas
drink till we're just good
enough to live in a houseboat
sail all our 2-for-1's down

the way

The Waveland Wide Open (The Shallow Song)

Have you ever been to Waveland?
put the ice chest in half water
400 yards from the shore
sometimes shallow aint bad

It lets the light get in
the mermaid merman
ziplock sandwich– the yes-nik picnic
with never a fear of drowning

Shallow as strings-
or- no strings
on a nerf football

If we had souls
we'd be soul mates
not just for the fall

No bombs had to go off here
to get us to delta bikinis
but there are many sets of steps
to nowhere
all along the Malecon

Knock me down with three storms
or something if you love me
get Betsy and Camille to help the new girl
ruin my ruins right
it's good to be shallow in light

of such matters

Shallow as an opener
on a key chain

If we had better
souls we'd be soul mates

This is where we listened to *Ocean Rain*
and learned to taint-slap Time
space between the beach and the road
and the music horizon
and all of us

An hour from the city
gets us to the fun-end of the line
just call it closeness
just call it spicy dewdrops

Shallow as crossed icing
on a warm bundt cake

If we had more soul
we'd be soul mates

Piers falter fine – into the decay
the lone and level sands stretch far

The spinnaker puffs out thin as silk
taut harp for sun and wind

Hands on the hull play their play
lone and level sands

We are shallow water
down for coda or cola
in the sun or moon or mud

Sparkly Blue Shoes

I think maybe
every seven years or so I howl

                            a ghost
                        and become
                        a new human

I can still play Battleship
on the porch
with a dagger in my lap

I can still sooth
our baby daughter
to sleep thunderstorm-through

and at the end of the rain

I can talk   I can tell you
                        what I want

but I'm not
fully formed
                I'm fully former

a fully flooded floor

I should probably go
to the gym on Canal

I need an ANYTIME kind
                    of fitness

that can Lazarus back after
canoes float from street-birds
back to bayou

                    I mean the moon
                            is a movie
                    showing for everyone
                        at a theater near you!

so perhaps it's better to stand
in front of a mirror
                        and flex

till tree branches switch reels
till I'm between scenes
till the baby is filled

                with her own family
                of ghosts

it's already easy to see

                    the past

        wave-crashing through her
        like eyes opening in her blood
            and I'm afraid

when she's past

running and jumping and begins

hovering

I'll have to tie a brick to her
sparkly blue shoes

because if not she'll become

a lost balloon
a branchy moon

something

the ghosts fly away with

I always hope
I can catch it happening

my ghosts I mean

skipping
down the hall
out my howl

just to whistle with them

as they go

sing the lies I love to live
but again the stale cigarettes
have signed us up

    for the table of shame

and when the baby sleeps
she sleeps through storms

because all the bottles
are empty
and my longest glance

    through gliding clouds

isn't long enough
to buy us a house

I tether myself
to the rented porch
chase a dagger-phrase
down the steps
        just to rip
      some cigarettes
    or get hipped

hide like a spider
      in a dream

but I deprioritize my health and fail

all relationships
                    with sleep

I think I'll think of a way

        to colonize
            a new New Orleans
                            on Mars

on the crass assumption
there's a better view

of the past

but then a jet flies through my view
of the moon
and I get all jangly

so the only thing to do

            is bug bomb the porch
                get rid

of all the tiny spiders
                I can't see

before the coast erodes
before I have to learn how

    to build

a barrier island
to loop back and become

                   a natural process

Marianne Moore Cherry Apocalypse

crumbles sticking
to skin

each jazz should smell good
or look pretty but not both

with the staggering bad news
one has to go with
"Life random" or
"Am cursed"– not everything can be
a fortune cookie crushed
in bed   into another fortune
in bed evading pleading home

it's not just sea through the sun roof
getting into the backseat

and flooding the submarine watching
along with the family drycleaner

that's the only ish
the kerning of the octopus
coral tabs on acidosis ocean
is the end of the playground

pretty soon you're gonna have to be rich
to get ANY of the good shit–

treatment   much less decent coffee

the spines of the celery already too hard

We're here
in Trinidad, Cuba
    ex
    clamation

the guys in the jumper-and-hat sets
are not Revolution reenactors

  but here to buzz the mosquitoes

& ripped a new one as only Cubans can do
by the lady purveyor at the door–
We're selling art here!
        Anyway no one's getting pregnant
right now anyhow!

somewhere between Collected
and Selected and arcane parlor

bets   we seat ourselves between
picking and choosing

  we line the wooden berry
  right there on the stripe

Dana play dough

She hates taints
    as much as I hate
'at the end of the day'

but right
out my mouth
just j'adore
    the octopus's   three hearts
    and blue blood

Can one be gruntled?
  enough at Karaoke Beach Tiki
to mike drop
 and make an instant
    ant lion's den?

We drew the souls of animals
        just as the Noahpedia suggested

 took the plankton for a walk,
                the doves for a good cry,
                and the bears for a 'season-siesta'

  we made whale-penii
        sno-angies [unavoidable]
    in the sand

our imagined weather-phenom
            the *Sno-cone-icane*

　　　　　seeded with nectar syrup
　　　taking the nation by storm

　　　　　　　　　　bringing the Year
　　　　　　　　Without a Humor Clause
　to a thump-happy
　　finale

　　　more twisty straws more radio
　　　more white hot blue clouds

The Panama Record

(sponsored by Throwback Cola)

you know the one where
the hairy no-shirt rocker
yells Pan-ama!
Pan-a-maw-haw-haw-haw-haw
(is it four haws, I'm not sure?)

It's an analogy for how money moves
(one crotch hemisphere over).
The old days – castle & gristle–
when you had to 'fill out
a record' with a tenth song

a lot of pop now just fills
the filling (coco-commotion donut)
would be better becoming material
and filling the sinkhole on Canal St.
that just keeps growing.

The Panama Papers
come in for a mention,
as well as Abe Vagoda, the Snuf-
alufagus, and Deep Throat.

Some things just sound
cool and some don't.

Follywood (Going down)

At our future forest jukebox, Dee's breasts
awe the Dothraki, Bambi runs away.
Jennifer Lawrence: I'm going to decay
like everyone else, wood goes on the fire.
Caressing the Internet's not the same
as Island Living, putting up a forcefield
with Brooke Shields' stiff upper lip
that rad banana-fetching monkey.

Oil slick spotted near wreckage site
along with body parts and luggage–
maybe being human alive terror [is].
Players used the tombstones as tackling
dummies, now needing neck pillows
and pickles. Don't we all need more pickles?

Keats is Not the Problem

is not the tag on the t-shirt shot
from the cannon

but I wanted to say— *Thanks,*

Custom Ink!

and have it on Brett's doorstep
before Brett
could canonize

              the masses meaningful

without them knowing
anything
ever happened

I'm feeling the right costume
cape and smile

could really move
the books

              off the shelf

but then again
the TV poet on *Transparent*

just said *lostness*

and everyone   applauded

maybe my gifts are best given
          in another world

     where we ain't afraid
     of no ghosts

where Brett tells a moving story

maybe the one
we've all heard
                    maybe the one
                    we've all told
maybe the one with the books
and not all of them
can go

          the one when the move

     from uptown
to tracks
     really gets clackin'

the one when every time Brett
says
          to Kamenetz
or maybe Kamenetz
                    to Brett

Keats is not the problem

something meaningful happens

MEANINGFUL POEMS

I walked under a ladder today

and I shit you not
shortly after   found a

ossified nougat   barge colored
lucky penny   to counteract it

trim into the cold
and only one glove

  kept my right hand warm   in her left jean pocket
reading the Koran akimbo   for the boring parts

made Keats my astronaut
to the Spanish Steps little planet   on the dogwalk

        in my mind

    because I realized there was no one
    to leave this song to

  a sort of double-echo
karaoke shower soapbox

It's always also-ran and runny in my New Orleans

            I went down on Life
        a theramin prosciutto hero

The day the mirror was my father

I thought Sarah was busy o-my-goding

    the noise next door—

    the scrape of neighbor against hood

but she'd just
o-my-god-ogled

Gentilly pics of shitty houses
we can still afford

till the gents get bored   raise the rent
above the bayou

if we don't move into the house
under the curve of that mid-city current
where the baby says
                   the monkeys live

I'll still be sitting here where
I've been since the day

the mirror was my father

        trying to make language
        dad-optional

trying to love the couch for all its stains

spring-loaded and trying

to squeeze

        all the *lostnesses* out

of too-tight blue jeans

When birds cry

the moon's below the horizon
        I think I just walked on it

autumnal crunch mixed in
my carnival summer-bag

on the other side of
Mardi Gras Mountain   being bionic

        by just being normal

I wish I had a dime
for every quit

some kite   across Brazil hills
 is my sound of music

  secretary for the other stuff
hired on the spot
out the gutter

The next time you see me

    I'll be up for canonization

right now I'm cannon fodder

feathers about the explosive parts

I am a dumb astronomer

single star I look to
for guidance
    (I didn't catch your name)

It was a night to take to
the porch because of
                a problem inside

then night man had to awake to another picnic

see where the family came from

how I went from child to old

spillway mudflat rivulets

of the snake track reunion

& then there's the Chee Wees!

    tilted on the short levee

  sun reached its hand down the front

 of her pants

 chip-clip fell apart
  in my grip

The door to yesterday

the pithy girlfriend ganja

fell me into the Anchor Lake campfire

        as if I was trees

  and I was off

in my time machine   (trusty head-saw)

   never slaying Adolf's

    vegans or dragons

but petting the dog

    guarding my personal demons

        (Simp & Hijack & Karma Chameleon)

I didn't ever figure

   outside this absent parent
   A-frame getaway

there'd still be gossip ghosts

around the portal of embers

taking chits on my exit method

Hey and yeah
   just because Keith Cucullu's a dick
   doesn't mean we can't be friends

but now

the now I

hula'ing this now   behind us some field

     watching two black holes

          demolition-derby

ripples across your ripaway jersey–

I'm just dust held together by longing

changing dry county by stars
to tryst

          the god of Chop the Mountain

   will be the one I later pray to

there goes the angel

that bird   with her amp

back upstairs

   the lake is willing to swallow

   us whole   so we stare   we pier

we go home on dumb wheels

when the machine stops bleaking

I broke free on a Saturday morning

on a Friday afternoon
to chew through the meaning of life
to knife *we're only human*

putting the pedal to the missing koan
Carrolton corner to corner
I followed the Demolition Diva
Oak St. to interstate
as far out of town as a peach
can reach its pit

the pink ass of the dump truck
(hers or whatever dude driving)
backed dump-up against my fender

fake it till you make it I slogan'd
to the rear view and radio
and invented in the absence of train
one meaningful clack to Baton Rouge

New Orleans and all its secret parks—
every clandestine peck
on the cheek a black satin rose—
bent behind me like a nameless lake

when where the flesh pales is a face
wifely about-facing to say
tonight and tonight *and* tonight—
it's murder it's murder—

till memory to mud

I'm busy trying to learn how to put
a peach back in the fridge
(once it's wasted) with untouched fruit
with the unbruised anything

but the fridge is funky with family
photos and wedding invitations
and all magnet letters are the colors
of babies' dreams

p.s. / there are dreams in this world
and the next

I'd forgotten my hand

had been asleep all morning
till my autistic student
making his mad shark loop
around the classroom
stopped to compliment
Michael Myers

to tell my desk that he digs
his coveralls and stealth
but doesn't care for the mask
then he weaved through
the girls in the back
talking of all their mall trips
and wardrobe choices

that's when I felt the tingle
again and needed a big
big hug—a floating dagger
to carve a rad path—
because I could tell I'd get
choked-up in chapel

                    because
I guess we all need love

New Yorker sailboat

in the elegant East River   not docking for poverty
taking on the cream
      of the American Dream

Aquila Danger is the high hired frisson

 as everyone flirts   with a glass of ocean

    and the app   for Mont Blanc style
autographs

making the topless
topdeck klatch   a julepy mint –
we're all killer captains

It's great to be shallow   out over such deep water

  it's an open shimmer   study body
   of contrasts

a regal pink   epic ice bag   pillowfight

    America the beautiful   can also be hot
make waves
  and smart
from all the tomorrows taken in
to just one today

Onshore   there's another neighborhood waxed

to make way for another   café vegan vampire

Out here   it's elastic and eternal

                        trim and jib and rigging

                (a lotta)   Yacht on top
frisky submarine

smelled Friday's flower

on Saturday morning

and wondered

will pancakes
and cartoons
one day be ancient
weekend tradition?

either way
it can't keep me from mistaking
streetlights for moons

turns out

dealing with the sun's deal VS leaving
work without curses

when I left yesterday   behind

for the weekend
wheel of fortune

I left Al alone in the lonesome clutter
of my desk

spiraling in the funk
of Frank Stanford's dreams and said

the snake doctors are yours now
      so he wrote it on the board

I carried the mercy card home
in my ass pocket

transferred a week straight from kakis
to jeans
      jeans to kakis

      because I can't bear the thought
      of laundry

because my new century man is falling
behind

soon   I whispered
   to the bright blood
      sleeping beneath my skin

any Wednesday will wash you
   in its light

but when Janis jaunted by

complaining
      of monster-rain rumors

I shoveled the dirt and worms
a newspaper and piece of trash
that looked like a snake skin
and all the cardboard stars
              that crash

                                        earth to earth

    away from the drain

                    but all I wanted was to plant
                       an ancient mailbox
                          behind my car—
                  bone of dino and bunny of dust—

and never leave
the house again

but then
      at the end of the rain

"bayou living" sounds like a new playlist
                   I could groove to

maybe meaningful poems could be carved
in the kayak floor—

                        a new order to be recorded
                     in historic waters

then we can plug the holes

with more meaningful poems
the same that sunk us

sometimes I do things   just   to feel flooded

just
                    o well

  we can always just say "let's just stay

forever
on the porch

             and forever"

next time my thought bubble

is showing
someone should let me know
before I feel
like it's okay to see the same
smart shopper
aisle after Breaux Mart aisle

Disappearing a Poem by Major Jackson

I have not disappeared.
The banquette is full of my clacks. The sweet
olive bereft of my thinking. The Vietnamese priest
prays over my fish, it's catfish,
just catfish fried, with no soul and made to
die for my fussy palate, my talky lips,
my tongue elegant as a constellation on high.
Just because Andrew Jackson was a total

dick doesn't mean we can't hang out
in New Orleans and get our best puns
and lucky dog buns and metaphors
tattooed on our secret places,
the juicy nooks that defy the crud-muddle
of general existence. I have not disappeared
according to my selfie and ussies
and the way my wife laughs back

at my jokes, not just here but also in Austria
and Sicily. We're so curious whether our ancestors
liked to do it on the ruins or the rocks,
which surely have not disappeared, delicate sea-
song to pair with the flutter mascara. Their stern smiles
have given us ballast, a volcano's magic hat
we keep falling in. When we halfsies the two parts
of a po-boy whose cross-section resembles smash

Pangaea, a delta of juices runs hand to elbow,
and in a place nearly disappeared by storm force,

everything seems seemingly normal,
and sturdy like a basket of reeds.
It's too bad everyone can't see what we see,
and resign their cash to a head of a pin.
When I fade into the Springtime taking the park,
we still have not disappeared, even though its Quaker
parrots question the sense of ever being inside.
It is then we belong to Toussaint's Southern nights,
which by now you have mistaken as something
gentle and not the other side of the mirror
sinking the scented lagoon. We no disappear.

In our pets we see the level of care
pressing further into the mysteries.
In a library in Palermo, on a plane of oval moan
Buenos Aires, under a pass where bums bon-bon
a controlled fire, I am held by a belt loop,
a zippo, and a polaroid flapping.
One burns a finely wrapped cuban, then sniffs
the scented box it came from, scouring for
the bitterball smell of Anywhere-but-here-istan.
I keep it all in mind like a late-night shaman.
I have not disappeared. I swish the amber
shadow of lady-lager and ponder
how hard it's getting out there
for a shrimp, gumbo made by the Brits
and all the oil-paint plovers
grounded for take-off [faraway stockholders].

When we tattle our dreams, we disappear.
In N.O.U.S.A you can get stabbed on a neutral

ground, the one with the milk crate chair,
but never ever disappear.

I live a life of sacred gags—
sign language ranting past the graveyard,
and my mind adores the good old days
when everything was shateria
hurricane erasure. At a glance from across
the room, I wear The Cure on my face,
which is eternal ephemera, whether
that's Rockette sunshine or you're just
kicking for the coffin corner.

Source: Roll Deep (W. W. Norton and Company, Inc.,
2015)
back to top
RELATED CONTENT
Discover this poem's context and related poetry, articles,
and media.
POET
Major Jackson

SUBJECTS
Living, Death, Life Choices, Marriage &
Companionship, The Body, The Mind, Love, Desire,

Activities, Eating & Drinking, Relationships, Family
& Ancestors, Social Commentaries, War & Conflict,
Travels & Journeys

BERRYMAN VS BERRIGAN: THE BOARDGAME

William Prince Williams

this is just to say I have eaten
the icebox – nearly everything in it –
loving her now so much more than when
truly mine   Something about the clouds
and her mixed in the barrow which–
bustled and freighted– barreled down
the mountain through saloon doors
leaving us all   raspberry glazed
on the back of my motorcycle
beside the chickens in the noonday
sun – so delicious so sweet and
so cold the moon – we did it
this is just to say
thank you for the funky time

My hangover equals your being black

childminders in Colchester can be trusted
with Mary Millington– Two Gretchens in
48 hours – one of them told me
Don't put "bowlegged stilts" in a poem
but "bs" are what my beagle employs
as we go on a walk after I'm back
from the trip ps/ the crows and the rain
are what's left of my beloved New Orleans
large, young Silver Female found at corner
of Prancer & Fiesta (for reals) as I walk
the streets in sympathetic tee shirt
(re. being hot) in the sunshine, that
first line was written walking my dog

Henrietta Longs for Meaning

I wish someone would call me and breathe
into the phone.

Someone pretty please move next door and
mail me a love letter.

Darn a sock with your meaningful fist just
to make me a YouTube video.

Purchase my plane ticket from dust to dust.
This doesn't ever seem to happen.

the hot planned parenthood girl looks hot

in her dark pink tee shirt – with or without
the bayou backdrop and the gator that was
the apple of Eddie's eye – float-yoga
at one's own risk, yo. rats, I forgot to
mention my Squat Your Plot anti-
resentrification scheme, thanks Janine.

reading Eddie Berrigan makes me think
"beer panic plunger" rue my elbows and
"Section 8 fourplex ay caramba dp".
something about being a man of dreams
pans Xxx on the keg by powder-paid homes.
more tragically, I've forgotten what having
fun is, and can only persist in these poems

Making Believe

I'm a real freak
     a memory

the young Henrietta that just couldn't
understand *no thank you*

you're awesome but

     more bitten up

than a chew toy
floating on the open ocean

but

I need your help with this

really

before I go crazy   before I sprint

through the exit music

before
     I can't open the pretty door

in the ugly floor

and all I learned is

meaningless

I really need help
getting murdered

                I need help
        being dainty in summer

I need to be okay with being dumber
I need

a crushed up cucumber
for this drink
                        I need

smashy-crashy fun

                        heated

from the inside out

to be unattended unafraid to be drunk
in a pool while the credits roll

just once someone please
tell your big god to slip me inside
            its sleeve
            sneak me

into the movie with the meaningful

end

Night-Man: Ep. 1

whale belly

thing is
if I want to be a real boy
I want to

If I want to be a baby I want
to pee and poop
I want to run in place
of *I want the sun*

I want armies of worms
to overpopulate my parents'
blue globe
cringing in the den

I want everything plugged in
I want Superman
action figures
to die every winter

I want to mean something
when I am
this many years

of something

Henrietta Still Life

everyone watches the same movies
so why does it matter
if I walk into an art museum

it doesn't mean I understand anything
about its meaning

if I understand anything about art at all
it is something

like those little mechanical boxes
that sit in the corners of art museums

which I don't understand but here I am
standing in an art museum

and soon enough I'll be
sitting in a corner I don't understand

I am not art but maybe something
near it—something
passed by— something like that

Henrietta did it, in the kitchen, with her dreams

Your blue eyes the color
of vintage denim.

Skin like a fancy fashion show
in your mother's kitchen.

Open mouth pretty
as an endangered moth

fluttering
into murderous light.

And your bare breasts the buzz
of gratuitous desire.

Crying just to see
if you can

you make meaning as if
it's movie night again in hell

but we have a heaven
of heroes and a CLUE board.

Let's dream like zoos
closed for the apocalypse.

O Henrietta! O Mother! O Meaning!

dear mother

after the bull riding incident

                          I was the drumbeat

I was the drunkest one
at the bar

I was needles in your belly

then a man handed me a flag
and told me to crawl on the floor

the werewolves found me
and stuffed me
                       in a house fire

I was swaddled
            in sunlight

I was handed over to the masses

they told me to tell an audience

stop all the madness
stop pretending
                to make meaning

just take a poem

from the pill drawer

Sectional Henrietta

I

when you wear your wolf suit to bed
I dream you deflower me

my waking world

II

your werewolf hair makes me horny
O your horny werewolf hair is
so horny
            not stiff
                        like dead
                                    feet protruding

but clumped
            not dumb
                        but wanting

grease   a flock of geese to nest
bleached-blonde corn rows

                                    every time
you stand on the bed
a cat sequined on a sweatshirt

every time you shake your wolf ass
a howling heard by neighbors

a mop that dries the moon

a spilled scotch

so pour me another drink
while your fangs fang
                              pop in

another cube of ice

make me unafraid you turn all the boys
just because
                    but me
you want to sex to howl to bite
(on accident)
              the vein that holds me

to this sun to this meaning to this
ice cream man music

this pacing up and down the street

                      in front of the house

where I will have always
grown up

this open window
this space heater this 70's nudie mag

lost behind the drawer of the night

                         table

bought at the antique shop and
found by us this feeling this treasure

such a treasure to not have to

hunt

        III

yes it's okay go ahead
                    I don't want

to be human anymore
                    I want

a big hairy wolf dick
and yes
        I want to thrust it

but I also won't mind the murder
of who knows who
                or their sun-red blood

or my good pants ripped
or The Finger frowning
            over his broken trumpet
when he finds us

                    asleep
                    in
                    the backyard

and laughs

at the crazy night
we must've had

just before he murders us
careless as clothes
                              thrown

                    onto an unmade bed

Henrietta's Delicious and Compact Body

you take so long
to love me
and it's all your fault
like a pearl necklace like
a lost contact case

I've been wearing contacts
since sixth grade
but there are things
you don't know about me

here's something
I know about you
you wear wild socks
I've been staring at them
all night

you are the girl on the floor
wearing a snuggy
you are the biggest piece
of dust

the way you rape
the environment is kind of
off-putting
but there is no such thing
as purely animal

there are boundaries

there is surgery
there is joining legitimacy
there is hanging there is

granting the incidental
fifty different ab workouts
and the sky distilled
till an entire species
is at a meaningful party

N.O.U.S.A. still life

Who loses

        a bag of orange chee-wees
        out the window

        whap!

        now just off frost orange
          in the road

I can just picture the action

        Who?

Hi-Lo baby=

the basis of all good

American culture. At least yr not

getting datdogged

in a gutter

by a daiquiri knife.

JOKOVICH

Speaking of which...French Open?
NOOOOOOOOOOOOOO!!!
What will happen with Steve
and the zesty kambucha barrista
roughly age-appropriate?!!!

At Last the Meaning of Halloween Stickers!

the bats still spread black
wings across the front window
on Thanksgiving day

cock couldn't

magnetic
Henge
is a bitch

Dear Boogaloos–

please don't take this
spot. I'll be right
back. I play a big
cello and have
a bad back.

accident

for a long time
I had a vivid

memory of bouncing
off both hard
and soft objects

Sunday

Police to Zulu

When the Wind Blows

(nuclear winter tipping point)

sing a simple song
came so hard

twas dubbed
                 "sobbing"

When the Wind Blows 2

(nuclear winter tipping point)

sang a simple song
came so hard

twas dubbed

        "sobbing"

        cover song
        runny duck

Night-Man: Ep. 7

when I'm in season
my shadow poses the problem

language shames the table

dictionary.com sings
                    my body electric
        I mean *my spumoni*

but all my ears hear

is
            hang'n ther   happy   bat
dis city   drunk wif   stuffed   grlz

the porch moth beam attracts

with its god-glow
with its die-finger

can't kill *me* though
                    right?

either way this here Henrietta's
a huffy muppet

thanks me well for the fellowship
then hovers leaf-like
in the rusted rays of the metal sun

vined in smothers

like a veiny whisper   like a wish
misplaced
        in a PBR bottle of butts

not to drown but to dream
of drowning

      but I feel saved already
        so what ocean is this?

apex detox

plain panic drain

a backup pair of jeans called

Hot Rod Yesteryear

Nothing Gets Between

Munchkin Howitzer

Hello Damn

[or going natal native]

Drop-Trou Bear

Crapping Sunrise

Salmon Facemask

Vincent says

she stays

and she goes

haha

but mostly stays

Ptzla

pepsi tennis zipper love audio

[O, You]

You flew all around
& you tired yourself
out, Mr. Feathers.

You turn your head
around & sleep on
yourself.

Night-Man: Season Finale

dearest Henrietta

there is   something

        we can't produce
      even in wet dreams
                          even when

we will the gutters to long
      for stars

our heads bob on
                          like meaning

fishing for a constellation

toward the far
                          something

or maybe the other

                          way around

hush now, Henrietta

night comes
with its quiet dogs
its bridge
lights lining
the river its heaven
that really did
exist its exit
its repetitious sound
its deepest fog
its shivering fires
its children
its ditches dug
into back yards its
front its list

Last Call

bar bathrooms smell
like the past

saying so when you leave

a stall will probably
get worried
laughs or faces

but with clean hands
you enter a conversation
about tennis

or the President
lacking in racking up
death-tolls

you may just remember
being tough
in high school gym

but this is where you are

at least Henrietta is
loving you

the Xmas after her brother's death

Henrietta cries before she cuts in half
the hamburger chuck.

In the window above her sink
the moon is a white wolf
uncurling in the cold.

When Henrietta stands in the doorway
the doorway widens.

The white wolf slinks inside
and yawns on the linoleum.
The Christmas wreath tilts.

The motion light flits in the dark garage
like a trapped bat.

Sooner or later life begins
at memory, she tells herself.
Between here and there

she'll keep shaping beef patties, depend
on meat and softness.

DEDICATIONS

Birthday Card for Momma

feeling like dealing
                        with all the bang

the but-it-ain't-no-thang tragedy
that bares its iPhone tit pics

                    and my failure to find
                    a flag for all seasons

is making me want to grow a rat-tail
to appendage a new disposition—
a point that magics a path
to the nearest mosh pit

                I'll sit in the middle
                cuddle a lost shoe

call momma to pick me up
after
the crash

in a parking lot of lost causes
and fifty little hipsters
hiding

cigs in socks from as many mommas

            my momma never let me grow

a rat-tail

even though the best kid
in the neighborhood had one so

               did the worst

Jeremy Nelson the big kid with
the big freckles
and yellow mouth

when he held me down
summer was ending

          he spit on my face
          I pawed
          the torn AC/DC shirt
          he wore
          every day

and guess-who-grandpa
came crashing through

          the screen door

ready for the war he missed
but I wished it was momma

fighting for my life to go on
missing a rat-tail
as long as that meant I could keep on

making meaning

(also looking back
memory says to wish: *he spit sprite*)

but if meaning's just the medicine
I'll sign
all my poems
moon-person of dreams

            I'll forget everything

until somehow momma
can't keep remembering to keep
rat-tails from whipping my neck

    like fiery freckles
          like a barrel
               of burning trash

maybe we all need a momma
to Western Union some party cash
and to save a bit to send back

            in her birthday card

In the Hopeful Future

—for Vince

when I picture you at a party
you are arriving

scraping a foot on the front step
you kick caked mud
from the toe of your retro Jordan's
on the welcome mat
whisper the word *Jump*
under your breath

domesticated as the dozen carnations
you carry where you used to carry
a dozen dead elephants
inside a dozen dead snakes

you pat your pockets
as if you never left home
feel for your phone and keys
your fire hydrant heart
the memory of your younger face
reflected in a red motorcycle
passing you by

what a pouring down outside
memory puddles behind you
what the hammer and hot blade of it
the chain and anvil of it

the devil and lesser devil of it

somehow you ended up on this porch
you say to yourself
the way a river remembers
the only path is to the sea it ends in
then ring the doorbell

I can't remember half
of anything I can remember

Weathering

—for Michelle

grief has always felt dumb inside me

dumb as drinking egg nog   no
dumb as slurping sky   no
dumb as gulping the river that walks me home   no

all of this   swirling
                         and now I see I must have been
 mistaken

here   in southern Illinois
under the unlikeliest of skies—
                         Xmas: 60 degrees and rainy—

like ice clinking inside Santa's busted skull

I sit clinking against the weather
of your absence

while the weather in my voice—
swath of your eye shadow   black
streak
a mystery asleep in the overgrown pine grove

(sleeping a sleep old as hills)—
                         half-moon howls:

Michelle!   —report?

I am on very low sleep
          so if I've already asked tonight I apologize

(it seems like everything is so everything

but I don't quite fit where you are
and it's a bit maddening)—
                    Michelle!
I must also apologize
for November
          —it has taken me so long to start again

I deeply regret but I am glad I feel   this way:
          because I try to pry open your eyes
          failing so tirelessly you feel at home
          here in my life

WHEN BIRDS CRY

—for Chris on his birthday

For your big day
we got you the time machine
you always wanted   paid for with your
                                        purple K & B credit card
                          reading CHRIST ROBERTSON

            we can finally make
            the Acadians and Arapahoe win
         and Gill Fenerty get quick to the edge

                        beating the balloons for Prince
                          or, right, make that doves
                            out and over the Ooh-Poo-Pah-

Doo

we're sending a car
as in *Wanda Nevada*
  or Revenge of the Titmouse
                                        we'll be tagalong royalty
                                        like the time after Jass
                          Fest up and down Canal

                    tossing a box of Blue Boys
              like doubloons   all the way
                        to the Turning Point Lounge

      classy aquarium and matching napkins inside

banquette action like you like
on the pork chop moon

Dorsey's on the radio
the tots are on the hibachi
Dr. McGilhecuddy's on ice

We're just waiting for you to get here
It's time   to have some more Time
more room to play
money bags gone tubing
more play in the lines

Crows (Bird Brawn)

No one knows
just how much

crows "like"
their day

except for maybe the
crow-ologist

(you see where I'm going
with this)

end credit music

walking soundtrack

almost like flying

Where the city   meets the water

with the one   concealing revealing

leaf of a park

we humans

sleep with our real

estate agents

in sheepwolf

clatter &

eternal

trial balloon

Coming right down Broad St.

another group/ personalized parade

with clean-up crew

– it's peanuts

the girl in the English country

leaves for the large black birds

that bring her back rural bling

carny treasure-trash

mish-mash   longing belonging

Sun   some rhinestone

(on a field
 last place   we'd look)

 they found and brought back

 her mother's lens cap too

Sleep-Light (Advice)

—for Josh

dear brother the trees
in our father's lungs are hung
with white sheets

rip them down one by one

by fist or tooth or sighing child
by pictures by eyeholes
by murderer's mug shots

if you stop to question the moon
it's already too late

to be a sun in that black
absence be a sum of fears of
being the son of his breath and

close the gate behind you

you strange lumberjack you
digger of drunken night you
forgetful fuck you

go into the monster's fistful of
sleep-light like I have done

Mother I'm sorry

your backbone slid

down the doublewide
kitchen wall

and surfaced from the sea of
your sigh

he came on purpose

to box your imagination
of what I should be

you
should be carved

a lithograph of incubation
buttressing the hatch

if *lithograph* was
another word for a sore
version of self

myself the residue

an exit
into the world which maps

without knowing what

direction to flower

according to the apple core
you created

a Disney World dose
of make-believe blankets
the want of a family

to be to be to be

ravenous as 1000 mothers
who find me smoking
a blunt on the church steps

and everything else
not a kid at all

not ten fingers ten toes

I am a manger
stranger

than any baby can king

April is the cruelest bitch

—for A.

I'm nicely fucked up
but this feeling won't last

so I write
"Didn't I see you at one

of the Feringpark Hotels?"
on this cute little sheet

and dream of our Burkina
Faso ren-dez-vous

where we play more rad vinyl
out the open window and laugh

at the tranny dragon kite
the proto second line

in other words I think

of you not every day
        but always

am such

        "slacker ants" – do you know this?
it takes the place of a car chase for us

tremble-emerald spiked high heels
and tat-hem mini shifting the gears

the cam-shaft drift
of the two-tone metallic squeal

only happens at the Overlook–
                    but it's so much more than a soundtrack

                    what gay guys do alone
                    in their apts with a Prince song

                    'hot sheet trade'
                      in the hotel business

                    White Dwarf/ Black Hole
                      on the celestial plane

                      & so we come to (Sha!)
                    and come on your existence

                    The leaving paradise mouth-feel
                      was in the last place we looked

April is the cruelest bitch 2

the expanding universe
& Amber's damaged
rollie bag
as jazzfest parking
placeholder
along with Andy's garbage
and the oak stick Frank
used once
for his Dr. John costume–

and so some call in
with the understanding–

but a lot of my peeps
are better at the weeping
than the wiping

in the pool learning
stroke development
back in the shallows
for the calendar shoot

on rubber land again
up the levee
by Cooter Brown's
looking at life

through Flock of Seagulls
colored glasses

pinky out
with the Curly Joe Pineapple decaf

sometimes they're hard–

it's been a hard month
hell yeah, the whole year
so I'm just leaning

on the sky
my will and testament

A Minor Confession

just between
you and me

I've been under the deck of a pontoon and felt

victory brush against my leg
in the dark water

and I told no one

look everyone I am the kingfish of the heart
taking a breath

and I have been this because of this

and I have been burning
my thumb with cigarette butts

I have been what the fuck

I have been a forklift broken down mid-lift
only to not have permitted myself

to drive around the corner

long enough that I am beginning to be the hat
left on the gear shift

but once I was the bastard son staring

at the sun like an army of toys
and I'd said *go to hell or go live in heaven*

with the flowery fools

now I want to stare at myself on a screen
singing Springsteen

out of tune

Corner of Screen Status Square

—for Dana

I don't really even know you
in a way that means much

but not dealing
with unfollowing the friends
on Facebook

I can't remember following
isn't keeping
the sheets sweaty

so I just keep getting updates.
You change a lot, Dana—

         Thanks,
              I don't

Arkansas Summer Chimera

—for Frank

dried up inside my name
the creek bed filled with fossilized
turtle shells
speaks its glossolalia
leans into a song
I'm forgetting how to forest

the summer we dumped buckets
of crawfish and turtles and minnows
into Jeremy's storm shelter
flooded with a week of rainwater
we dumped buckets of snakes
into both our mothers

barefoot on blacktop the race
to the sun stopped dead
every night
when we washed our feet
before dinner with the garden hose
while the creek quieted

The De-Civilized People

—for Nik and LAX

I looked out on my country
and saw an airport
had taken over–
the food, the dress,
the bad TV with the sound
off, the neck pillow walking.

If there were ever best minds
some screen-sick bunt younguns
'sitting on' sitting on
unbeknownst to self and selfie
be cutting a fart on.

People are going to the polls.
Those with any money move
to the last four 'authentic' dells.
No one is bosky.
Sex is a breath mint.
That last line is fluffy and mean-
ingless, like the people or polls,
unclear which.

I'm going to church.
Not of the poisoned mind,
but of the pre-poisoned
pork rind. Camden Strong
is Queef Song.

My jeans still rock.
I haven't yet cut my cock
off and thrown it at the back
board. Out the window a vast
peaceful empyrean with clouds
outmuscles The Country.

At the airport
the people are some sad midpoint
of locker room sweat and grounded
spacecraft. Pardon our progress.
Lick our collective kickstand.
We'll be right with you.

Getting Away with Everything

—for Rebecca

if you're lost
after the first five minutes
of *Solarbabies*
like a haunted hallway
stuck between two time zones
"like" my orb on Facebook

let's go I don't know

where?

let's staircase down
dog-squeeze and tunnel-under
the lost and found
box at the end of that hall
start a band called Future Shark
throw ourselves out the bar

let's go I don't know

where?

getting your star chart read
surely's opposite
of shipping off to war
but since we can't all do that
let's pin a white sheet

let's project *Solarbabies*

till we find I don't know

meaning?

like maybe Jami Gertz's bangs
flaming in space?

Bereavement Myth

—again, for Michelle

though we've never touched
I pledge allegiance to the image
of the hand holding yours
as you run from the movie theater
through pouring rain

I have faith in a philosophy of blood
late evening brings

here your backyard angel
braids her blonde hair by the pond
at the bottom of the hill
paints her nails with blue eyes
wings and fur

I name the story of this noise nightly
until there are no more

lit with windows white as bone
the moments of your life I long for
float out on the pond
behind your ghost like ghosts
that have become my pets

I believe in the history of this dream
that never happens

The Twilight Zone of Caves

—for Andrei

halfway between the bats
and the entrance where
the twilight zone greeted the deep
dark zone in song
you might have said you were trying
to become a tree

I stood behind you
as that dark door in the face
of one of your caves
seemed to slash slowly open
as if all it ever wanted was
to let in a single shaft of light and you
its only Romanian on all fours

you said you were trying
to become a tree
or maybe this thin light of you
moving in my memory
mingles with what slinked
through that hill of trees
behind the fancy cabin you called
your modern hermitage

that was the kind of light you can see
only at night with night-eyes

so I can't really be sure
if you said you were trying
to become a tree
in the cave where you crept
just ahead of me and Vince 30 years
younger and trying to keep up
because there were no trees

just cave
damp stone
the distant drip of water
that cold cave smell
but that's always where you are
when I tell myself this story
crouched down allowing
every bat in your Romanian accent
to spill black into the branches
colorless as the cave-

tree you became

Moon Ending

—for Tonelli

the world was weightless
as a hit single

so I had to sit outside
so I had to sit out America
so I had to sit out AWP

Hollywood Circus Edition

and spit in a bucket
closest corner of the porch

trying to pretend I can tie
the clap that kills
the light to the lies I sing

but my weirdest eyes are

blued in tonight and things
look American

any good news on that side
of space exploration
any finished sandcastles

ready to face a worse wave

than these bad brain days
all this happening

and un-happening—
so sorry to be so untied
but here's what I learned:

birthday poems are born

under a certain moon glow
that kills gravity slow

The Gumbo Party

—for us

the night is fucking in the trees
was where I wanted to begin
three days ago this portable July
when I finally arrived
to the new pad back in New Orleans

but three hours into the trip
after acceleration ceased in Arkansas
the Lepanto wind made me
pee on my shorts

though the omen was engine smoke
told me it was time to sit
eat the Bill Callahan sandwich
bought back in Carbondale

(does Bill really eat jalapenos
on his sandwiches?   ...shit)

either way the dog slobbered
on the seat next to me as I imagined
him laughing: *those co-op hippies*
in southern Illinois would name
a sandwich after Callahan

the car started after half an hour
with nowhere else to go I was going

down south to mamas 50 miles
to shop the Nissan if needed
to let the dog and cats keep cool

I got the limp-mode-go-ahead
from the mechanic with his uncorded
code box free of charge
but that tacked on three hours

at midnight I bit the mid-city curb
two wife-beater dudes
pumped sewage with sweaty tattoos
and chain-smoked

the monster-pump-noise was more
meaningful than the smell

that was a Thursday and now
post-move eve with all the boxes
staged in the living room I need
Sunday smiles for my cemetery mind

so here comes Rom the Hare Krishna
humming while he glides
from Esplanade's corner temple
so amazed by the empty dog crate
I place on the porch by the chairs
last tenants left behind

somewhere under Rom's bare feet
something must be bubbling

through the roped opening of his robe
because every word for everything
I've ever carried is whittled down
to a beautiful   awful: *what is that?*

    (pause)
        I'm Rom

too neighborhood-newbie to face
the free-dinner Krishna-crowd
I slice smoked salmon and decide
I'll re-watch Game of Thrones Season 1
till Ned's head's lopped off or
the Esplanade birds stop murdering

if I was Kevin Young maybe I'd write
a poem titled "The Gumbo Party"
about the mid-city folks flocking by
maybe I'd read it on NPR
and someone would say something
meaningful afterward

but because I'm not Kevin Young
every time I reach for my beer
I think I hear a bird
in the bushes beside the porch
but it's always just my shirt
scraping against one of the chairs
the last tenants left and
the night fucking in the trees

Bonus Track

in bridge traffic
suddenly sympathetic

                I realize I too

have started mornings
with kites
made of lead

so I go into the next room

                    and write
                these lines down

because we need
to cross this
like a night skin
lullaby

because discerning gods
somewhere outside the window
orphan moonbeams
for all to gawk at

the land of the living
and the clouds
are someone else's problem

we are shallow water

when birds cry
as if I was trees
we no disappear

O well

says the biggest piece
of dust

O well

an exit into the world
                    a TV
        with the sound off

these ghosts
getting away with everything

                have become
                    our pets

black dinosaurs
with a list of band names

                and a pocket full
            of Admit One stubs

we don our night caps cuz
Keats is not the problem

just saying to the after-parade
                    I'm Rom
the Sunday after

requires no maintenance

requires only a night
                    of the living

and an appt.
with Misters Feather
                gets the Core Log
signed
and hires

lifeguards of the shallow end

cuz we love!
bubbles AND tears!

we cry   HUMAN ALIVE!
our friends   and fears ARE!

we know unfloaties
will save us if picking fruit
with pliers can't

either way   ghostcards

                        are good

    starter dirt

                        hold you

    when the music
    is not quite
    over

About the Author

BRETT EVANS is a Scorpio who loves pho and ferries. New work from the distant past will appear in the anthology *The Collected Explosive Magazine*. He is the Poet Laureate of Gentilly (a neighborhood of New Orleans, the laureate part self-declared). Work here with Boatswain Shipman continues his long love of collaborating with other poets, such as with Tracey McTague on *Owl,* Greg Fuchs on *Steaks of the Buddha Cow*, and with Frank Sherlock on *Ready-to-Eat Individual* (also from Lavender Ink). Two new carriers-of-the-flame in his house are named Sissy and Bonzo. With these two, he still searches the land looking for his lost Aztec Camera fringe jacket.

CHRISTOPHER SHIPMAN is author or co-author of six books and four chapbooks. His work appears in journals such as *Cimarron Review, PANK,* and *Salt Hill,* among many others. His poem, "The Three-Year Crossing," was a winner of the 2015 Motionpoems Big Bridges prize, judged by Alice Quinn. *A Ship on the Line* (Unlikely Books, 2014), co-authored with Vincent Cellucci, was a finalist for the Eric Hoffer Award. *The Movie My Murderer Makes: Season II* is forthcoming from The Cupboard in 2018. Shipman lives in New Orleans, where he teaches English lit and creative writing to high school kids.